Joke Book
by Artie Sprengel

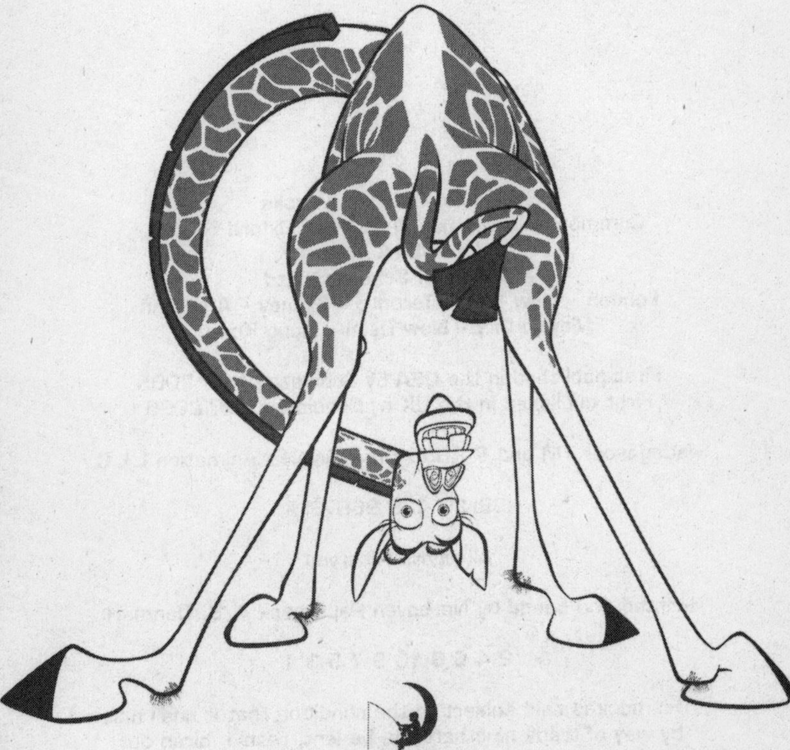

Scholastic Children's Books
Commonwealth House, 1-19 New Oxford Street
London WC1A 1NU, UK
a division of Scholastic Ltd
London ~ New York ~ Toronto ~ Sydney ~ Auckland
Mexico City ~ New Delhi ~ Hong Kong

First published in the USA by Scholastic Inc., 2005
First published in the UK by Scholastic Ltd, 2005

Madagascar TM and © 2005 DreamWorks Animation L.L.C.

ISBN 0 439 96078 9

All rights reserved

Printed and bound by Nørhaven Paperback A/S, Denmark

2 4 6 8 10 9 7 5 3 1

This book is sold subject to the condition that it shall not,
by way of trade or otherwise, be lent, resold, hired out,
or otherwise circulated without the publisher's prior consent
in any form of binding or cover other than that in which it is published
and without a similar condition, including this condition,
being imposed upon the subsequent purchaser.

Madagascar 8697 miles

gift shop

antarctica

9365 miles

grand Central 1.1 miles

ice Rink 0.8 miles   The Wild 13,996 miles

Alex the Lion's Least Favourite Jokes

Where does a lion bid for food on the Web?
ePrey.

What's a lion's favourite magazine?
Feeder's Digest.

What do you give an angry, bloodthirsty lion?
Lots of room.

What's a lion's favourite American city?
Savannah.

How does Alex do his shopping?
On-lion.

What is Alex's favourite US state?
Mane.

What does a lion press most often on his DVD player?
Paws.

What's a lion's favourite dessert?
Lair cake.

What was the lion Little League baseball team called?
Cubs.

What song plays at a lion wedding?
'Here Comes the Pride.'

ZOO BREAK!

Where do penguins like to swim?
At the South Pool.

What kind of bird knows how to write?
A pen-guin.

Where can you find hippos?
It depends where you hide them.

Why do zebras like old movies?
Because they're in black and white.

Why did the lemur buy two tickets to the zoo?
One to get in and one to get out.

Where do penguins keep their money?
In a snow bank.

Why did the penguin go to the South Pole?
To visit Aunt Arctica.

Animals' Guide to Using the New York City Subway!

Dear Friends:

Your first subway ride may seem scary. But with these dos and don'ts, you'll have a safe and pleasant journey!

DO use the handy metal swingers for getting around.

DON'T be careless sliding on the smooth seats.

DO take advantage of the walls for that last-minute hair check.

DO use the extra-wide double door exits.

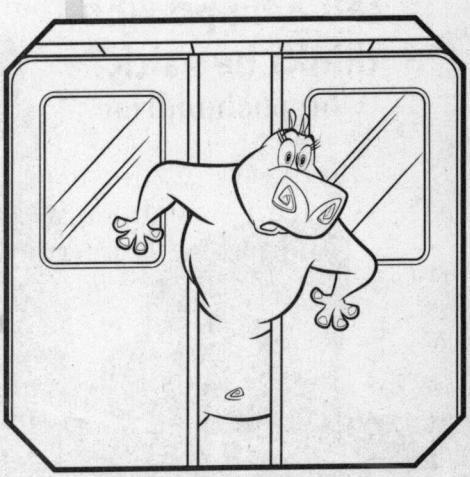

DO express your thanks to the friendly human passengers, always willing to give you a seat!

A Humongous Helping of Hilarious Hippo Humour

By Gloria

What do you call a hippo who thinks he's sick?
A hippochondriac.

How can you get a hippo to do whatever you want?
Try hipponotism.

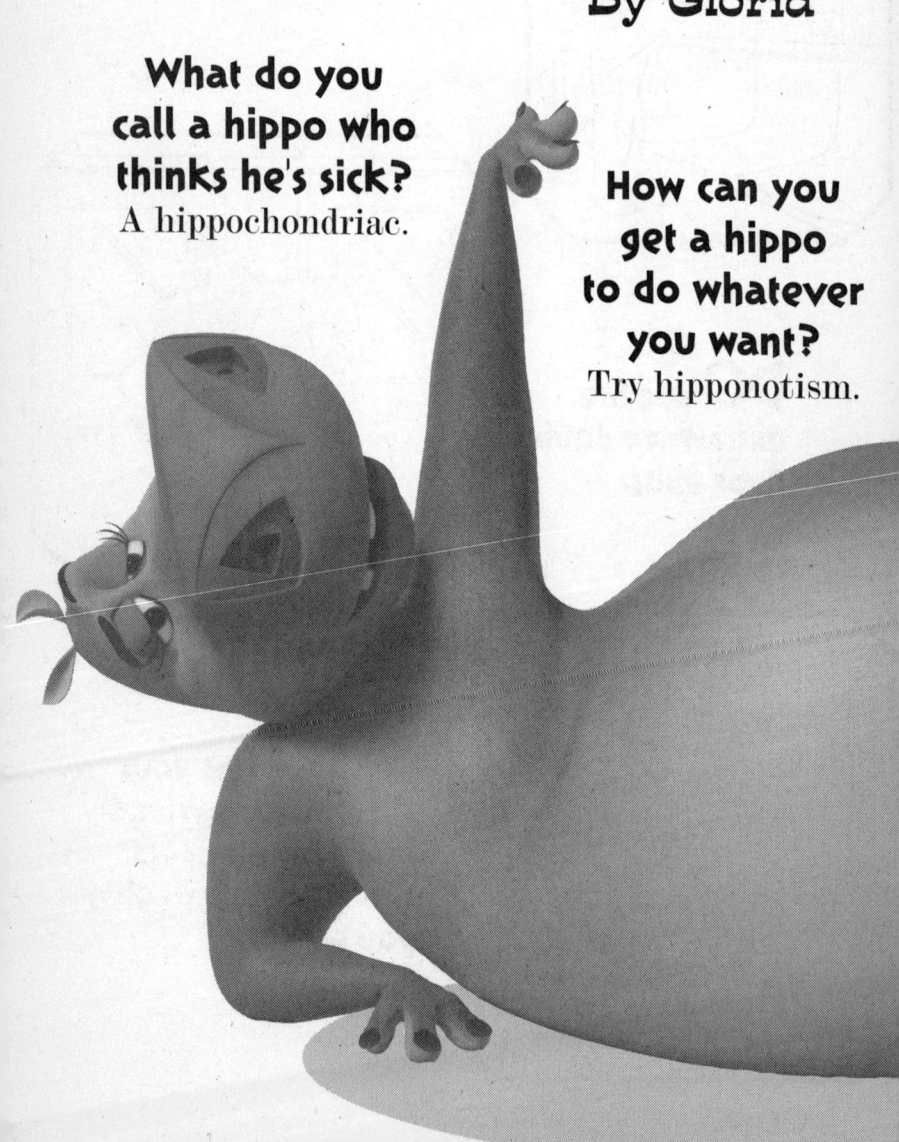

What loves peanuts and goes boom! boom! boom!?
A hippo skipping rope.

What is Gloria's favourite kind of music?
Hippo-hop.

What do you give a seasick hippo?
Lots of room.

Why do hippos paint their toenails blue?
So they can hide in blueberry bushes.

Wait a minute – I've never seen a hippo in a blueberry bush!
See? It works!

Alex's Gift List

For Gloria, the prettiest hippo in town:
the Alex the Lion souvenir pocket mirror and comb set (keep you looking gorgeous, Glo).

For the penguins, the craziest birds in the zoo:
the Alex the Lion souvenir beach bucket and spade (to help with your digging).

For Marty, my best friend:
the Alex the Lion souvenir stuffed animal (that way you can take your best friend everywhere).

For Melman, my tall friend:
the Alex the Lion souvenir umbrella (the weather gets bad up there).

For Phil and Mason, two smart monkeys:
the Alex the Lion souvenir coffee mugs (I know you love your morning cup).

Alex's Instructions for Tourists at the Zoo

DO admire my mane — ALL THE TIME. A lot of people worked very hard to make it look this good!

DON'T say "Here, kitty-kitty-kitty." (I HATE that!)

DO remember to buy Alex-themed souvenirs at the zoo gift shop!

DON'T — under any circumstance — say "Ew, he smells."

DON'T use flash photography... unless proper conditions have been met:
- 'Good side' is exposed to viewer (lion's LEFT-SIDE only!)
- Mane has been licked into a proper heroic 'do'.

DO throw gifts of appreciation. Flowers are fine, candy is dandy, but meat can't be beat! (Filet mignon or T-Bone preferred.)

DO applaud wildly. If you like Alex, let him know! (Lions are people too. Or whatever.)
If recording Alex, **DON'T** upload without permission. Roar-sharing is illegal.

℞ Tips from Melman for a Healthy Lifestyle

Be sure to avoid:

Limes
They cause Lime Disease.

Germany
Another way of spelling 'any Germ'. Coincidence? I wouldn't risk it.

Exercise
Remember: there is no fun in athlete's foot fungus.

The Bronx
Most likely sour[ce] of bronchitis.

One bercul[osis]
It may lead to t[...]

Hospitals
They're full of sick people!

Clocks
The tocks are [...] but tics can [...] disea[se]

ATTENTION, SAILORS! I have found that you birds have the poorest knowledge of nautical terms used by yours truly, the Skipper. For your enlightenment here is a technical glossary, ***to be memorized immediately!***

Amidships – correct response: ***Gesundheit!***

Bow – what the captain's dog started to say, before we decked him (see deck).

Deck – to knock out (as in ***We decked the captain***).

Galley – another way of saying ***Gosh***.

Gunwale – something we must not do; they are an endangered species.

Halyard – part of familiar greeting, ***Halyardoin'?***

Hull – we don't use that kind of language on my ship, sailor!

Ice floe – ***Hi, Floe, I'ce Skipper***.

Mason's Mildly Amusing Monkey Musings

Why do monkeys have fur?
They'd look funny in plastic raincoats.

How do you fix a broken ape?
With a monkey wrench.

What is Phil's favourite cook[ie]?
Chimps Ahoy.

Why does an ape wear sunscreen?
To get an orang-u-tan.

What is the first thing a monkey learns in school?
The Ape BCs.

Why won't Phil visit his cousins?
They live way out in the baboon docks.

LEMUR IQ TEST

Approved for general use by
King Julien

Match the question on the left-hand page to the correct answer on the right.

1. How is a coconut like a banana?

2. What did King Julien get when he spilt his milk down his front?

3. Which side of a Madagascan animal has the most fur?

4. On the way to a water hole a lemur met six fossas going the other way. Each fossa had three lizards hanging from its neck and one crocodile following close behind. Each crocodile had 23 dragonflies on its back. How many animals were going to the water hole?

5. How many lemurs does it take to change a lightbulb?

a. What's a lightbulb?

b. The outside.

c. Wet.

d. None. Are you nuts? The lemur ran away.

e. They're both brown and hairy, except for the banana.

Answer key: 1. e; 2. c; 3. b; 4. d; 5. a

Score:
6-7: Smarter than King Julien. You will be thrown to the fossa!
4-5: Moderately stupid. You're working too hard.
1-3: Congratulations. Total moron. A credit to your species.
8-10: ABSOLUTE IDIOT. You can't count! Congratulations!

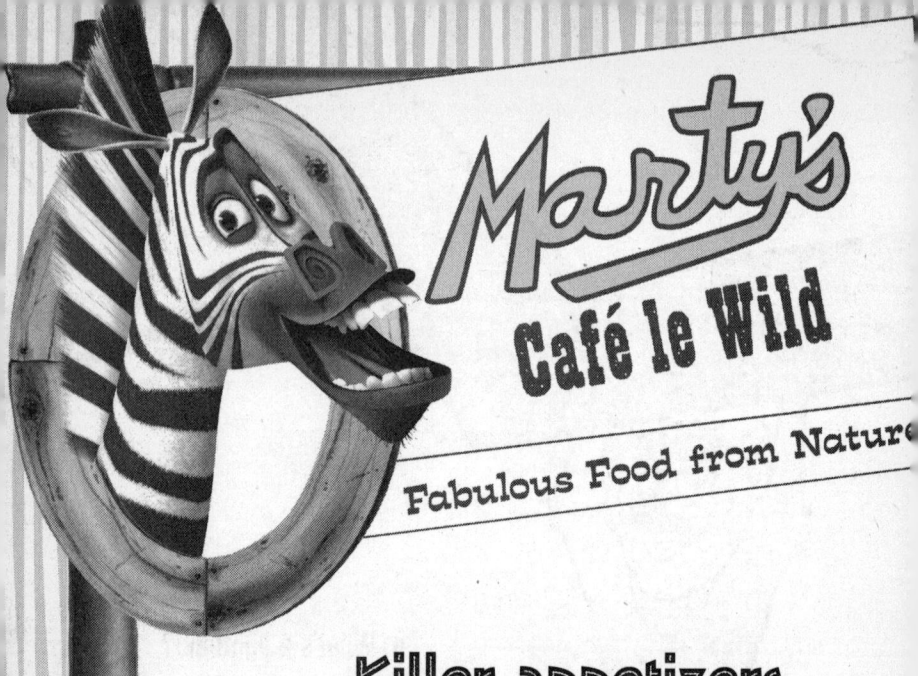

Marty's Café le Wild

Fabulous Food from Nature

Killer appetizers

Old-fashioned Seashell Grits
Carefully crunched overnight, then simmered over a flame and served with coconut milk.

Going Bananas
Shredded banana peel dumplings (with or without saltwater dipping sauce). You'll find it's always a-peeling!

Succulent Seaweed Salad
Served with clam juice dressing.

Crack-a-lackin' main dishes you never had in the zoo

The All-Natural
A selection of grasses sprinkled with Madagascan topsoil.

Leave Your Senses
Tender hand-selected leaves on the branch (with spicy jungle fronds upon request; specify 'mild' or 'wild').

Jumbo Insect Chowder
Made from a hearty stock of humongous winged wonders, trapped in standing water and aged at least nine months, then cooked in tree sap, and seasoned to chewy perfection! A meal in itself.

Delectable desserts

Crunchy Sand Cookies
Try 'em before you love 'em!

Hair Today, Gone Tomorrow
Our patented coconut hairball puddings. (Nothing better for digestion!)

Melman's Sick Jokes

What do you get when you cross a giraffe with a hedgehog?
A six-foot toothbrush.

What do you call a ten-foot-tall giraffe?
Shorty.

Why are a tree squirrel and a giraffe best friends?
Because they often see eye to eye.

Who won the giraffe race?
I couldn't tell. It was neck and neck.

What do you call a giraffe artist?
Stretch-a-Sketch.

Why didn't they invite the giraffe to the party?
He was a pain in the neck.

What does a giraffe always feel before anyone else?
Rain.

What do you get when two giraffes collide?
A giraffic jam.

to the New York Zoo Giants

Gloria: Goal keeper; not afraid to get down and dirty with her opponents.

Alex: Striker; nearly impossible to sack; would rather eat leather than kick it.

Marty: Sweeper; speedy; used to wide-open plains; no hands.

Melman: Wide midfield; on extended sick leave.

Phil: Full-back; prone to monkey business in the backfield; nineteen banana-peel-on-the-field red cards this season – one more will lead to permanent MFL (Madagascar Football League) expulsion.

Mason: Wing-back; able to read the defence; in the last game he read them to sleep, then took the ball and scored a goal.

Skipper, Rico, Kowalski, and Private: Central defenders; flippers allow for patented knock-out defence; can be used as footballs in emergencies.

The Jungle Expert
Advice for Confused Jungle Animals

Helo,

Moreess Mawrice thinx hee iz sooooo smart. But I'm the King. Me. Just ME!!!!! Sumtimes I think heez laffing at mi. And then hee maks evybuddy else laff at mi to. Am Eye two kind? Shudd I lash them all 30 times on the but With the tale of a ring-taled leeemur?

Sined,
~~Anonni Unonym anonymuss~~ Sumbody

O Wise One,

I'm not the slimmest of animals, okay? Now, I just know they all talk trash behind my back. Like, "If fat were money she'd be a billionaire," and stuff. I want to smack 'em, but my mama taught me to turn the other cheek. What should I do?

Love,
Hippest of all animals

Dear sirs,

I am new to the wild. The weather stinks, the ground is slippery, the leaf quality is tough, and I feel sick. I came here in a crate and there's no going back. My friends tell me I complain too much. Do I?

Sincerely,
Long-necked herbivore from New York

Transmitted by Ship-to-Shore Communiqué

SOS. As leader of the Fighting Force of Fine-Feathered Fowl, I confess to a most dastardly dilemma. Having commandeered a mighty human vessel, we have obtained our goal: we have cast off our shackles and found our ancestral home! The whole place is full of our kind – a Penguin Paradise! But we hate it. It's cold and snowy and windy. What should we do?

Everything in Black and White

What's black and white, black and white, black and white and black and white?
A penguin rolling down a hill.

What does a penguin have that no other animal has?
Baby penguins.

Private's Comedy Corner

What do you call the floor of the penguin's ship?
A poop deck!

What is black and white, waddles, and has flippers and a trunk?
A penguin going on a holiday.

What's black, white and red?
A sunburnt penguin.

What does a female penguin wrestler do to her opponent?
Flip 'er!

King Julien's Rules Fit for a King

1. Be fair.
If attacked, let fossa have equal access to all subjects.

2. Be decisive.
In the case of #1, run!

3. Be wise.
If the ground is brown and soft, tread lightly. If it smells, let Maurice go first.

4. Be in peak health.
Eat fruit, lots of fruit, TONNES of fruit! I LOVE FRUIT!

5. Never forget a thing.
Do intensive memory exercises three times a day.

6. Be sure to always... um...
Wait. I'll think of it...

How do lemurs catch fish?
By holding their heads underwater.

How do they hunt birds?
By throwing them out of trees.

Why did the lemur cross the road?
Because the chicken scared him.

What has big eyes, fo[ur] legs, brown fur, a low IQ and is found near th[e] North Pole?
A lost lemur.

Is it true lemurs are halfwits?
Only the gifted ones.

How do you keep a lemur from smelling?
Put a clothes peg on its nose.

Lemur FAQs

Courtesy of the cutest lemur of all...
that would be me, Mort!

What is the lemurs' favourite book?

A story about a lemur crossed with a teddy bear: Winnie the PU!

What do you call a fly in a lemur's brain?

A space invader.

Do lemurs make chocolate chip cookies?

No. It takes forever to peel all of those sugar-coated chocolates.

What has black-and-white stripes and keeps going round and round?
A zebra caught on a merry-go-round!

What's black and white, black and white, black and white, white and white?
A zebra in a snowstorm.

How do you get down off a zebra?
You don't get down off a zebra.
You get down off a duck!

What's black and white and green?
A zebra with a runny nose.

What kind of animal is a zebra?
A horse behind bars.

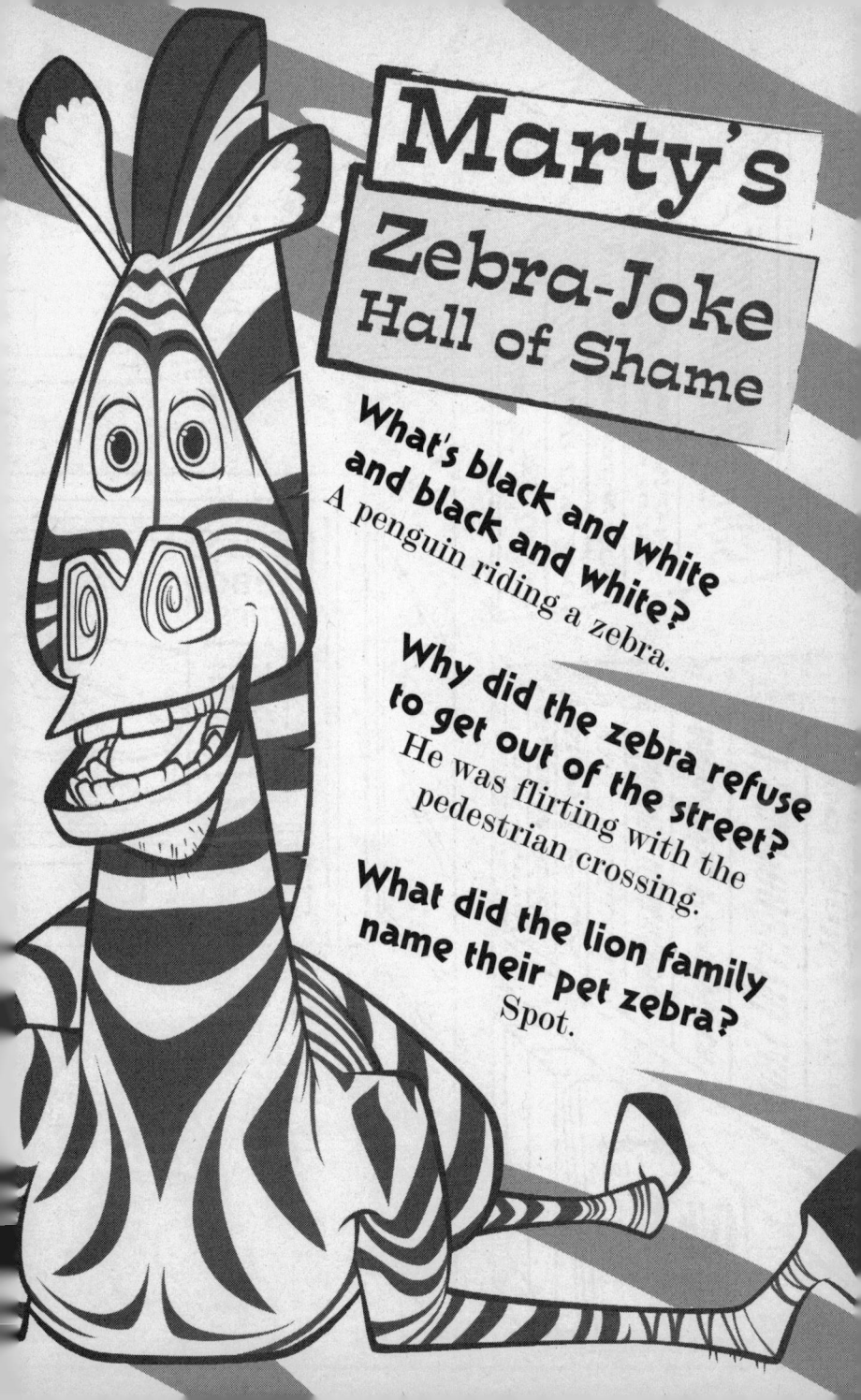

Marty's Zebra-Joke Hall of Shame

What's black and white and black and white?
A penguin riding a zebra.

Why did the zebra refuse to get out of the street?
He was flirting with the pedestrian crossing.

What did the lion family name their pet zebra?
Spot.

CAPTAIN'S LOG

At last I write of the penguins' plight,
A tale that's sad but true:
Despite the sights, life really bites
Whilst living in a zoo.

With spoons we scraped – and thus escaped
Beyond our prison gates!
(Well, we tried . . . okay, I lied:
They shipped us out in crates.)

But oh, the fire of sheer desire
Gives penguins awesome powers!
We clocked the cap'n, who was nappin' –
His mighty ship was ours!

We set our sails through tropic gales,
And worked till we were sore.
No rest until we reached our quest:
The cold Antarctic shore!

And lo, one day, across the bay
I spied it – what a hero!
My mates said, "Sir! The temperature,
It slipped way under zero!"

We came, we looked – and then we booked!
Perhaps you know the reason.
Though zoos are whack, we're headin' back –
This lousy place is **FREEZIN'**!

Alex's Message in a Bottle

Sirs or Madams:

A secret code is in this note. I know it's not
Very subtle, but look, I'm in big trouble. My
Ex-best friend, this zebra? He had this incredibly
Mad scheme that made absolutely no sense: "Let's
Escape!" he said. But the point was, let's escape
From what? Was life so terrible in the zoo? We
Ran around our cages, wowed the crowd and put
On spectacular shows! What a life, huh? But no,
Marty didn't think so! He got us shipped away from
This joint, and off we went in wooden crates over
High seas to a place I'd never even heard of. It has
Every inconvenience ever known and I really
Wouldn't be surprised if this place violated the
International Animal Rights Agreement. Okay, so
Listen up, whoever you are, and send help on the
Double!

What does Alex's secret code say?

Answer: SAVE ME FROM THE WILD.

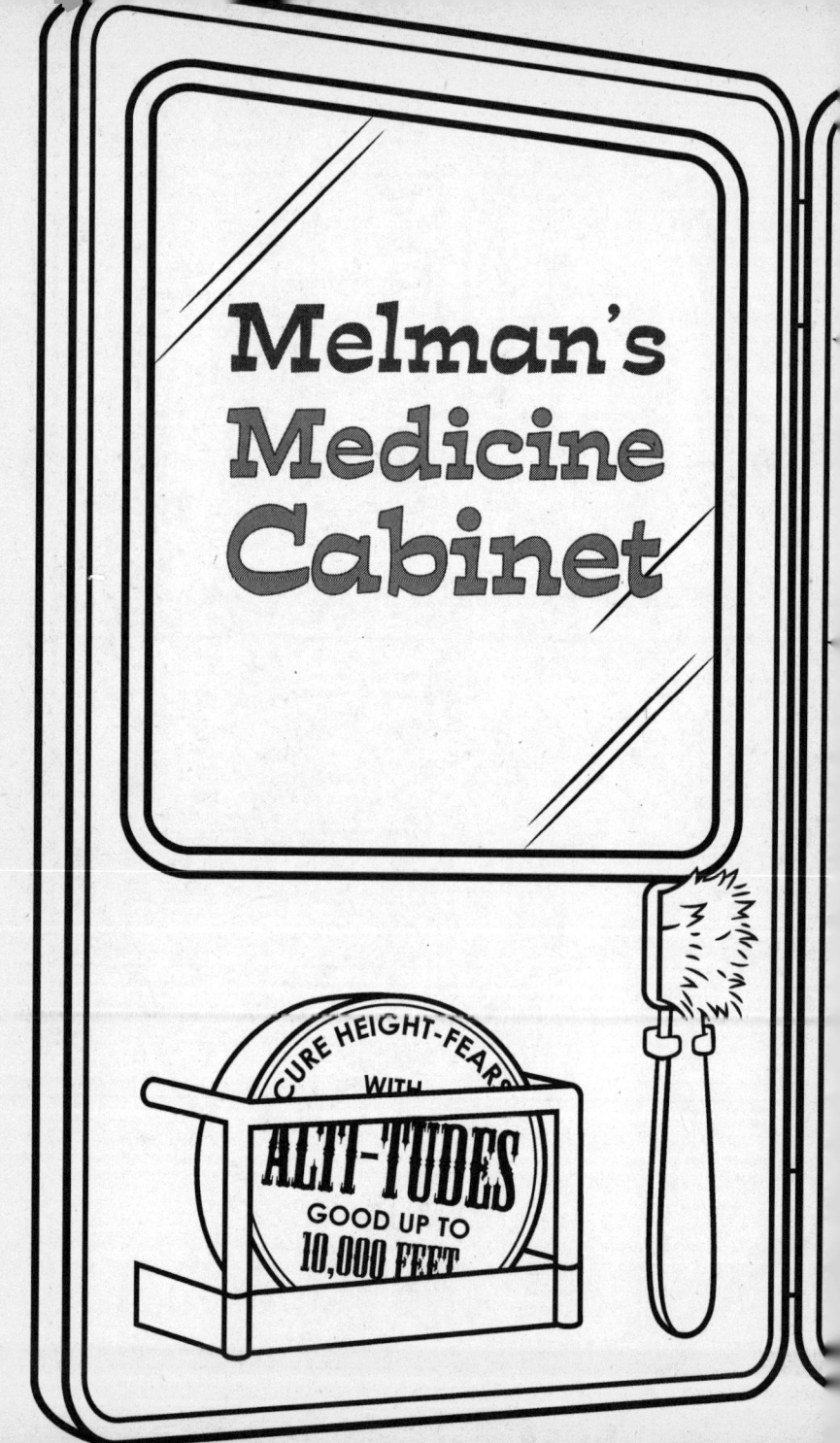

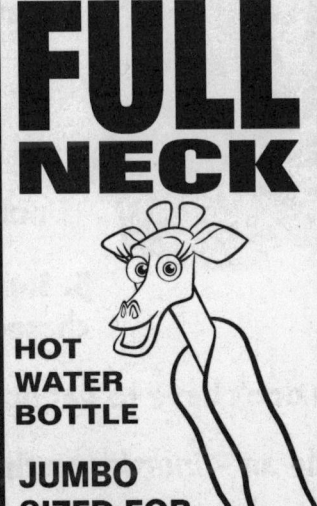

Alex's Top Ten Reasons Why the Zoo is Better Than the Wild

10. Squirrels are cuter than lemurs.

9. When was the last time you saw a taxi in the wild?

8. Or a mirror?

7. Night life is more than just mosquitoes.

6. No one in New York ever heard of a fossa, and I like it that way.

5. The jungle is too quiet.

4. Horns should be heard, not seen.

3. Steaks should be served, not chased.

2. You don't have to eat hot pretzels to love the smel

1. Jungle air – *murder* on the mane-do.

Marty's Top Ten Reasons Why the Wild is Better Than the Zoo

10. The natives don't speak with New York accents.

9. Lots of fresh water. No more leaky taps.

8. The things flying overhead actually flap their wings.

7. No one says, "Hi, horsey!"

6. Somehow you don't mind the fur coats.

5. No flash photography.

4. Running on grass is a lot better than running on a hoofmill.

3. Fruits from trees taste better than fruits from trucks.

2. Stripes stay in fashion all year.

1. Lemurs may be weird, but they know how to PARTY!

KNOCK KNOCK JOKES

Knock Knock
Who's there?
Alex!
Alex who?
Alex Plain Later!

Knock Knock
Who's there?
Marty!
Marty who?
Marty glad to see you!

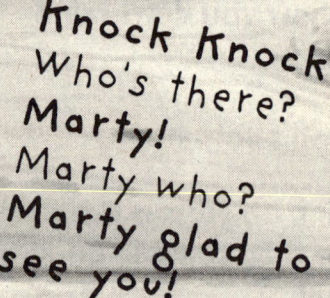

Knock Knock
Who's there?
Zookeeper!
Zookeeper who?
Zookeeper away from me!